COLOURED VIEWS

Poetry Unraveled

To: Cameile
From: Joseph
Read, Share, Enjoy!
June 2024

Written By

JOSEPH EDWARDS

Insta: @dipeoplespoet
Email: jdocforreal@gmail.com

ISBN: 9781777485948

ACKNOWLEDGEMENT

I want to say special thanks to all the persons who assisted me in completing this book.
I thank the editors Lauren Venson and Jessica McCurdy-Crooks.
I also want to thank my Graphic Designers who have done an excellent job with providing the appropriate images and layout for the book.
For all the persons who have consented to their photographs being used in this book thank you. Special thanks to the Flemmings, and Sucki C.

Finally, I want to acknowledge Bogdan Dirică, Gavin Allanwood, Jonathan Borda, Chris Gallagher, Kelli Tungay, Veřejná doména, ArtisticOperations, Eberhard Grossgasteiger, Axiomgenius, Pixabay, Hong Jiang, Prateek Katyal, Tumisu, Katrina Wright, Jude Beck, Michael Longmire, Pham vi công, Max Kleinen, v2osk, Olya Kobruseva, MustangJoe, CMElixirs, Gyorgy Szemok, Drpepperscott230, Caique Silva, Michael Anfang, Elisabeth Wales, Fran hogan, Pezibear, Fauxels, Timur Romanov, Robert Collins, Alexey_ Hulsov, Aqib Shahid and Jude Beck for the images and photographs used in the book.

Contents

Introduction

An enthralling experience awaits you, so indulge, and gobble up the words from an author who delights in giving his best. **Coloured Views** is a rich authentic blend of poems. Infused with a sound knowledge of the Jamaican people, their lifestyle, and personal experiences as shared by the author.

Drawn with words, this collection of poems is a beautiful collage representing the diverse culture, yearnings, and exploits of a nation.

Of course, the book wouldn't be truly Jamaican if highlights of victories wrought by some of our greatest sons and daughters were not chronicled, or achievements of our brightest superstars not mentioned. All these and more are woven between these pages.

Kudos to those who will read this book and find it inspiring and entertaining. Note, it's for all there is no age limit. Encapsulated in each poem are waves of emotions spanning; longings, outrage, humour, anger, dejection, jubilation, frailty, serendipity, hope, pride and reality.

Read, enjoy, and share!

Master Bolt

On your marks, get set, Bolt!
The hero and legend of the track is at it again,
He may smile at the start, but he is not your friend,
That engine of sublime speed, perfecting his torque,
Like a flying bullet releases its' Concord sound, not even the powerful Gatlin could chamber this single round.

From Beijing, to Berlin now Rio his base,
Different continents, new challengers, but the same result in every race,
Different lane draws but none affected his awesome pace,
Lots of competitors hyped up, but left in utter disgrace,
Quietly in the end they were only saving face,
For him nothing has changed, it's always first place.

Smooth as a dagger ripping past some muscled flesh,
Cutting asunder dreams and hopes, taking more never less,

He takes it all like a jeweler adding gold to his chest,
Like a purposeful party-crasher leaving masses in distress,
One more medal down for him it's just a show,
For challengers their place in the upcoming race they already know.

Maybe it's fate or just his destiny,
Maybe it's by design for one man to be,
Master of the track, just as Jordon mastered the court over time,
Tiger Woods mastering the green, and king Pele a football magician for all time,
Ready, set, go! These races and games you really cannot colt.
On your marks, get set, go!
Uhm, you know I meant Bolt!

Bolt Again

Bolt again! mi a tell you mi fren, No matter ah which race, Him ah guh end up innah first place, Record or not, him jus bun up di track.

Once upon a time Gatlin did a speed down to the finish line,
But Bolt jus flash pass him quietly and tek di race dat time,
DeGrasse, poor young lad, him did a try a little thing,
So Bolt haffi spread out pon di track an show him di eagle wing.
Ah nuh one time massa an ah nuh two, Di big man haffi warn di both ah you, Unnuh fi understand unnuhself especially unnuh medal place, When unnuh enter di track an di big man innah di race.

Now dat di Olympics dun, Bolt is back to his usual fun, Di party Vybz high an still tun up, Drinks still full up innah di big man cup, But its business time an drinking dun,
Anytime ah nex race fi run,

Chattabox bwoy, unnuh free paypah bun, Cause Bolt pon di track ago melt unnuh like butta gainst sun.
Next Olympics might be fi unnuh time, Because by den di big man would have already resigned, Three consecutive Olympics, with eight shiny gold medals, He's untouchable in sprinting, even if yuh put on pedals.

Ballad:
Jamaica Big In Beijing

It was in di month of August 2008,
When a likkle island called Jamaica go inna big big China go mash up di place,
From the day the Olympic team touch dung inna Beijing,
People from all 'cross the world begin fi say dis ago be a big thing.

Di water cube and di swimming was good, but we neva feature inna dat,
All good tings did come at last,
di day di Jamaicans touch di track,
The stadium was called the bird's nest and di Chinese was right bout that,
It was the place the fast like bird, Jamaican performances were hatched,
And di wor'l was given a few quick heart attacks.

Dem get heart attack?
Yes! Crowd a people mi a tell unnu di trute!
Because the ongle ting dem coulda si was di bottom a lightning Bolt boot.
Di record him go bruck inna very quick time
He did that glorious feat in just 9.69

Can you believe dis?
Dem jus a recover from dat,
When di three little birds give di big eagle a major heart attack,
Di hundred meters for women, was truly the powerhouse time to shine,

So yuh can just imagine when Jamaica step up and mek a straight line,
One! Two! Three!
The commentator him was wrong,
It was One! Two! Two!
Inna the bird's nest bangarang.

They thought it was over but we had only just begun,
We were making a statement to di worl' Jamaica is number one.

There was a certain record considered a super-human feat,
What then would you call a man if that record him could beat,
I don't know about you but this is what I saw,
A lightning bolt flashed from the blocks and the entire field plus record destroyed.

I should have told you it wasn't pretty,
To the competition Jamaica was a dreadful sight,
Because we took all top sprint medals, and oh yes! The records dem bite,

Melaine and Veronica come after but dem join the party soon,
In a blaze of glory they sent people crying back to their locker rooms.

The performances dem so good that pon wi athletes dem start to tek set,
But check the facts again, a neva we did mek di bird's nest,
I am from Jamaica, and I can tell you this is true,
Wherever you find a bird's nest a wasp nest is nearby too,
So when yu approaching the bird's nest mek sure yu steps them right,
Cause yu have some likkle yellow wasp and them nuh romp fi bite.

To those who speak proper English,
What I meant is that the wasp will sting,
So do not be confused,
the line before is only a Jamaican thing.

We have no president here,
But our prime minister was very right,
We can achieve great things,
If Jamaicans just unite.

There is a lot to say but I could not continue to write,
By now I guess the world has seen this tiny country's light,
By the time the Jamaicans fly out of Beijing, all di gold medal supposed to dun,
So fi di next Olympics our athletes like Usain, Sherika and Asafa, should collect nothing less than platinum.

Jamaicans Dem A Superstar

Jamaicans, dem a superstar,
If yuh bawn pon Di Rock, yuh riches caan deh far,
Wedda you bat or yuh bole, yuh run or yuh sing,
A centuries an' records, an' a trophy thing.

It nuh really matter, wah you waan fi do,
From a Yaad yuh seh, mi bredda jus be true,
Easy nuh sista mi know yuh have Voice too.
Wi tek di worl' by storm, inna a US show,
And if dem "Tess" we again, wi a go mek dem know,

Fi wi thing no normal, di limits dem high,
Check Racers Club; dem ting touch di sky,
If wi run a one race the record drop brap,
If is a group ting star,
Di other man ting flop.

If we sing a one song the Billboard it a top,
So wi tell dem again, say wi just naaw stop,
Ask mi no questions, mi tell you no lies,
Jamaicans a superstar,
Rasta would say yes I.

The Hunger Games

Hungry for more, I went searching
having gotten a taste in Beijing,
then a mouthful in London,
So I dared to dream
about having a three course in Rio.

Hungry for more, I will not sit relaxed looking at others,
because their meals have long lost their appeals,
mine will be lined with mineral ingredients not unwanted substances from a deal
It will be mined out not created through laborious means.

I will be fed at the front of the line,
the place where the world can see me just as it was designed
just remember when I'm served first
that like everyone else I joined the line, be happy for me
I paid my dues and not a fee

After all I'm neither greedy nor am I puffed up
never using strange masked products and never stuffed up,
I'm just trying to satisfy this burning hunger deep inside my gut
Its been nagging me for the past four years
Causing me to ponder sending me to bed in tears.

Salivating at the aroma from the kitchen I quickened my steps,
Yearning to taste the Brazilian cuisine, to see the Samba chef,
while reminiscing on the soothing English teas I got,
and the tasty dishes from the Beijing, China bot
I'm looking forward to Rio, back broad, chest bare,
Because I'm well aware look the Amazon, it's a jungle out there.

Di Heroes Dem

The Magnificent 7

Marcus Garvey, him a wi hero,
So is Nanny, Sam Sharpe too,
George William Gordon and Paul Bogle.
From Stony Gut, St. Thomas mi a talk,
Fi di heroes dem mek wi walk!
From Stony Gut, St. Thomas mi a talk,
Fi heroes dem mek wi walk!

Norman Manley chose the politics,
Alexander him fambily was a part of it,
But when Bustamante go form him own thing,
Wi get a two party system,
Trumpet still a blow an' di bell start ring,
From Stony Gut, St. Thomas mi a talk,
Fi di heroes dem mek wi walk!
From Stony Gut, St. Thomas mi a talk,
Fi heroes dem mek wi walk!

Di heroes, dem a call wi fi stan',
Why yuh hol' yuh head dung, and yuh belly it ban?
From Negril Point, straight to Portland,
Mek wi start di change inna fi wi islan',
From Stony Gut, St. Thomas mi a talk,
Fi di heroes dem mek wi walk!
From Stony Gut, St. Thomas mi a talk, Fi heroes dem mek wi walk!

Jamaica Love

Jamaica the country that I love,
The country I love to hate,
The place I was born,
The place many innocents die.

The hills, the valleys, the plateaus, the plains,
The gullies, the tracks, the short cuts, the lanes,
Our wants, our needs, our losses, our gains,
The laughter, the smiles, the groans, the pains.

The crews, the gangs, the deaths, the births,
The cities, the slums, the ghettos, what's worst?
Our sun, sand, crevices, and sea,
Our vision, our victories, yet villains roam free.

We have athletes, artistes, musicians, diplomats,
Your legacy is rich, it highlights what you've got,

To your shores your offspring brings prosperity, renown and fame, But after sharing so much worldwide, why so little gain?

Many like to see her banner raised high in the sky,
Others exist only to detract and draw poverty nigh,
I cry for Jamaica, she's like a woman abused beyond words,
I hear her groans for mercy when her dignity she tries to gird.

Still, many love you, and wish you success,
A few still mislead the masses, and create a perennial mess,
But you'll be delivered oh Jamaica, from this wicked path,
If men fail to help you, it will take God's wrath.

Di System (Dub-Poetry)

(Merit Award winner – JCDC Literary Competition)

Di system, dung a yaad yah nuh right,
Di system, a gi the yute dem a fight.
A di system, mi a tell yuh bout yute,
Di system, mi a tell yuh di trute.

Inna di system, no wuk nah run,
So di system, full a drugs an' gun.
Tru di system, nuff lyfe cut dung,
So di system, my yute a nuh fun.
A di system, mi a tell yuh bout yute,
Di system, mi a tell yuh di trute.

Di system, it full up a pure trick,
So di system, cause problems like dis.
A di system, mi a tell yuh bout yute,
Di system, mi a tell yuh di trute.

Inna di system, not even food we can buy,
Di system, a mek mek nuff people cry.
A di system, mi a tell yuh bout yute,
Di system, mi a tell yuh di trute.

Di system, set fi di big man,
Pon di system, is ah destruction,
Di system, bring war inna town,
So di system, it need fi tear down,
A di system, mi a tell yuh bout yute,
Di system, mi a tell yuh di trute.

Di system, teach divide and rule,
An' di system, determines who get schooled,
Di system, a mash up di nation,
Yes di system, dem new religion,
A di system, mi a tell yuh bout yute,
Di system, mi a tell yuh di trute.

Dis yah system, yah ah gwaan too long,
Dis yah system, wid dem two party song,
Bout di system, nobody nah sing,
Cause di system, pure failure it bring,
A di system, mi a tell yuh bout yute,
Di system, mi a tell yuh di trute.

So di system, it need fi correct,
Cause di system, a lead di country to wreck,
Di system, it haffi change one day,
Di system, yow it really stay a way,

A di system, mi a tell yuh bout yute. Bout di system, yuh jus hear di trute!

Tax Again

Tax again!
Ah caaaan tek it mi fren,
Dem tax mi pay last week, now dem tax di piece a lan',
Dem tax di cooking gas, now dem tax mi minivan!
A wah mek dem a drop it so?
Time tuff like stony grung,
No wonda people caaan tek it, an some sick and tumble dung.

Tax again!
Now dem demand it from the dead,
Dem no get a likkle time fi R.I.P. or relax dem head, Him gone
lef di house, but still in the red,
Transfer and property tax fi pay, a dat di authority said.
Him lef a likkle ting inna di bank, fi help grow him yute,
But tax chop off di interest mi a tell yuh di trute,

Tax again!
A wonda if politician pay dis,
A wonda if dem know how it feel,
when food price thump you inna yuh belly like a hard fis',
You go buy a small food, and yuh hear a big price,
An when you check it out, dem say tax gone pan di rice!
Yuh cyaan even drink a juice, worst if it taste too sweet,
Cause di tax pon di suga high all di cane faamah dem it a beat,
Yuh han' dem dutty but yuh cyaan barra no hose,
Cause di way water tax ah run, it soon run pass Bolt.

Tax again?
Politician! Unnuh try fi barra less,
Unnuh nuh think dat deh policy wi lower tax,
even if ah nuh di bess?
Wi hav' sunshine every day,
"So How Come" we a pay so much fi light?
Wi tiad fi see tax pon certain bills!
Unnu naw listen or hear poor people plight?

Unnu still a tax di people dem?
By di way, fi unnu tax pay yet?
No wage freeze di people dem unda still,
So dat no jus mean more debt?

Wild Wild West

Western Jamaica has become the wild, wild west,
What's happening out there, is anybody's guess,
The police are trying, but heartless guns are barking still,
Each morning you awake, another person is senselessly killed,

What's causing the violence?
Nobody really knows
But with each passing hour,
the security forces are kept on their toes,
Criminals in the west with clean guns and dirty cash have made a link,
Pushing the very lovely city to a painful and chaotic brink,

Some say its drug running, others believe it's just gangs,
Some say its tuft war happening, others think it's a clear reflection of Babylon,

Many blame lotto-scamming, a few say it's the politician's fault,
However, you look at it and see their efforts are coming to naught,

What is your point of view?
It may be better than mine,
Because like Port Royal of old the west appears to be sinking in crime.
Henry Morgan is now dead, but did his spirit move west?
Western parishes today resembles the deadly pirate's nest,
So how can it be fixed? This time patch and go just won't do,
It's citizens time to rise up and cause the gangsters to fear you.

Living Di Life

Dem lovin eh, dem a enjoy life,
Dem nuh dwell pon di pain and sorrows,
Dem nuh practise fi fuss or fight,
What a way Mary treat John good,
A di best pair inna di neighbahood.

She respect the man yuh si, and yes baaba,
Di man love him wife,
This yah match make inna heaven,
Da couple yah did choose right,
A nuh everybody lucky so fi get a good spouse,
Some pick some partners,
Only God knows what dem bring inna dem house.

Every morning yuh wake up is a fuss,
Before yuh go sleep is another fight,
When di nagging a go stop,
Will there ever be a candlelight?

No time fi sweet words and hugs,
No time to laugh or kiss,
No time fi complement each other,
Tell me a wah kine a relationship dis?

Mi a tell unnu di trute,
Mary and John ting, it look sooo sweet,
So before yuh continue fi live like puss and dog,
Pack yuh bag and hit the street.

Chatta-Box Bwoy

How yuh talk so much likkle man,
give yuh mouth a break,
yuh story dem nuh credible,
di worl know say dem fake,
bout yuh travel regula,
a doubt yuh know di airport,
tell people say yuh own big farm and speed boat,
when yuh know yuh don't own a she goat.

Yuh a jus 25, but yuh look like 49,
young man, go feed yourself,
get a wuk, and stop waste time,
everyday yuh deh pon roadside,
a wonda who a pay yuh bill,
a talk bout yuh a bank manager,
yuh right, fi the river bank a Guys Hill

How yuh so lie likkle man
how yuh chat so much bwoy,
what yuh get from doing this
yuh naw go stop fool roun,
till one day yuh get a real hard lick
Every woman yuh waa hol' on pon, bwoy,
to you every skirt tail look di same,
yuh no see di woman dem know yuh game
tell me where is yuh shame.

Young man pick up yourself,
jus try a thing man, even become a farmer,
cooh roun yuh, look pon land!
Bwoy, it look like yuh really nuh have nuh ambition,
shut yuh mouth chatta box bwoy,
go find a job and stop complain,
and fi di last time mi a tell yuh,
stop disgrace yuh family name.

Indignation

Indignation, indignation! It jus ah eat me out,
From mi core to mi trunk like a cancer ah sprout,
Indignation, fi di wickedness mi si all aroun,
Whey a blanket fiwi Jamaica from Skyline Drive to Pollyground,

Indignation, indignation! It jus ah eat me out,
From mi core to mi trunk like a cancer ah sprout,
From Westmoreland to St. Mary even Clarendon it reach,
Across Kingston, St. James now ah Portland inna de hot seat,
St. Catherine eva warm an one time Manchester did cool,
Now St. Thomas and Hanover under the same murderer's rule,

Indignation, indignation! It jus ah eat me out,
From mi core to mi trunk like a cancer ah sprout,
Pure stabbing an shooting an murder every day,

Ah wonda why wi hart suh dutty up and tuff like refine clay,
Every likkle argument end wid annadah death,
Is like wi luv fi go nigh-nite more than party or fete,

Indignation, indignation! It jus ah eat me out,
From mi core to mi trunk like a cancer ah sprout,
Wi naw act civil, wi behavah nuh right,
Is like some vampires wake up pon wi,
Inna broad broad daylight,
Machete blades jus swinging an gunshots book their flight,
Is like some people join a Buddy pass system wid Madden's an Brite-Lite,

Indignation! indignation. It full mi up to di brim,
Indignation! Indignation, what piece a sin thing,
Dem luv morgue an cemetery more than dem luv go ah gym,
Suh nuh baddy nuh safe again inna dis bloody system,

Indignation, indignation! It jus ah eat me out,
From mi core to mi trunk like a cancer ah sprout,
Unnuh fi wash unnuh dutty hart, and purge unnuh stain up soul,
Allow di country fi prosper cause too much innocent head a roll,
Di land deserve a break,
and Jamaican people a cry peace,
Mi indignation is just a plea fi tell di killers fi cease.

Guns, Grades, Girls
(Gold Medal winner – JCDC Literary Competition)

Guns, grades, girls, is this what life's about?
Guns, grades, girls!
I feel overwhelmed, I feel like I could shout!
Why have the fear of guns damaged so many places?
Why do illegal guns terrorize so many faces?
Why are the guns filling community spaces?
Why, after its use, it disappears without leaving traces.

Guns, grades, girls, is this what life's about?
Guns, grades, girls!
I feel overwhelmed, I feel like I could shout!
Why have the grades left so many without a space?
Why have the grades caused us so much disgrace?
Ruining our race!
Why have low grades been with us so long?
Why am I hearing the same sad lack of education song?

Guns, grades, girls, is this what life's about?
Guns, grades, girls!
I feel overwhelmed, I feel like I could shout!
Why have the girls been brought down to this?
Controlled, compelled, punished by their abuser's fist,
Why are educated girls living without a job?
Can't we see that their dignity is being robbed?

Guns, grades, girls, is this what life's about?
Guns, grades, girls!
I feel overwhelmed, I feel like I could shout!
I think venting will help, in controlling pent up rage,
Reducing toxic anger and setting the stage,
To destroy all illegal guns, vouch for better grades,
To uplift our talented girls, to begin a new age.

Ole Denture

Mi say! Di denture pitch out,
Right outta Mass Zeekel mouth,
Him get a joke, couldn't hol' it back an buss a big grin,
When mi look inna him mouth no teeth, ongle pure skin,

Di gum still deh inna place,
but not one tooth withstood di marathon race,
Years pon top a years him a nyam tuff cane and yellow yam,
So di teeth dem decide say dem naw tek it no more suh dam,
Dem all conspire to retire hurt,
Di day him reach 71 according to him fren Burt,

On that fateful day, one by one him teeth dem drop out,
Til a ongle soso tongue an gum lef inna Mass Zekel mouth,
Him hol him head an start fi wonda, if a crosses deh pon
him,

Or if inna life him did commit a double dose ah di
unpardonable sin,

Truth be told di teeth dem glory days did dun,
So dem yellow instead ah white an fade den disappear like di
settin Sun,
Not even a likkle off white,
Fi mek dem look kinda bright,
Suh unfortunately it came down to one sweet joke an one
big grin,
to dismantle and show up di overwork denture system.

Tek Care a
Yuh Yute Nuh Dawdi

(Part 1)

So tek care a yuh yute no dawdi,
Nuh yuh bring him come?
Mine him no pawdi,
Hey, why yuh lef di burden pon di mawmy,
So is a nexx man yuh wah di likkle bwoy call dawdi.

Real man tek care a dem yute,
Dem thing eva straight, dem stan absolute,
So nobody nuh haffi ask, who a di fadda?
Nuh mek nobody ask, who a di fadda?

It nice, making baby sweet,
But memba pickeny have to eat,
No mek nobody ask, who a di fadda?
No mek nobody ask, who a di fadda?

No, it wrong, nuh tek jacket sir,
Yuh a big man, mek di suit yuh prefer,
Back to square one, pause, as you were!
Suit out a son, suit out a daughter,

Suit fi look slick, not a jumper,
Suit fi fit yuh, not yuh brother,
Mek madda proud, hail up yuh father
See you get a twin, now that's much better.

(Part 2)

Real man nuh run lef dem child,
Start hide or gwan like dem wild,
Dem eva present fi guide dem son,
Fi dem yute can pick up nuh gun,
Back to school stuff, dat sort out,
Rules at home di bwoy caant flout.

Daddy please, tek care a yuh girl,
Treat har nice, so she fit fi di worl',
One day she a go have baby too,
What a ting if di baby daddy just like yuh!
Suh tek care a yuh yute nuh daawdi,

Nuh yuh bring him cum, mine him nuh pawdi,
Why yuh lef di burden pon di mawmi?
Is a nex man yuh wah yuh likkle bwoy call dawdi!

Style Har Miss Lou

(Gold Medal winner – JCDC Literary Competition)

Easy yuhself young lady
cause yuh no ready fi dis,
Miss Lou is not a newbie
suh your ignorance is not Bliss,

Miss Lou inna category by harself
ah suh di ting set long time,
Suh gwaan ah Merica wid yuh dutty behavah
an tan inna yuh naked line,

Try yuh bess walk fass galang
or book di next outbound flight,
Cause yuh fi know Bandana cloth
even if yuh see it inna miggle nite,

Ah A-class Miss Lou inna
yuh even know wah dat mean?
An ah which class you kum outta
fi think say nakedness tun yuh inna queen.

Coovah yuh heart bun wid kin teeth
Yuh cyaan win dis yah time
Yuh tablecloth comment out of order
and gone way outta line.

Jamaica's cultural icons are revered
Miss Lou is jus one,
So be careful how you tread nexx time
Fi avoid di bangarang.

Pedestrians Lament

Traversing our roadway is a daunting task,
Is following the road code just too much to ask?
Most drivers today don't seem to care,
and in the hearts of pedestrians they're driving fear.

Passengers and pedestrians left dead in their wake,
School children among the lives reckless drivers takes.
Bikers without helmets like Daredevils on wheels,
left breathless on the roadways was that really the deal?

A pedestrian's lament begging you to amend your ways,
Beginning today, it may extend your earthly stay
Whether riding or driving practice to do the right thing,
because death, pain and sorrow, is all reckless speeding
brings.

Disasters

Nuff disaster deh yah inna di earth,
Suh mi ear dem say from di day that mi birth,
Hurricane, earthquake and volcano,
Flooding, bushfires plus tornado.

Towns and cities completely destroyed,
Disaster jus a deal wid eeh place like a brand new toy,
No matta weh yuh live or weh yuh try hide,
Disaster wi bruk dung yuh door, an fling all yuh roof one side.

Hurricane Katherina invaded di USA without fear,
Volcano erupt an bun up Montserrat an Hawaii mi hear,
Tornado liff up house, bus, truck, car and van,
Tsunami sweep whey cattle, hotel, an a whole beach inna Japan.

If mi neva see Hurricane Gilbert 88 miself, mi woulda say a lie,
But a nuff big roof lift off and tell di house an dem owner goodbye,

Some tried to catch their roof but they almost died,
Di hurricane lef dem a look worried inna di clear blue sky,
Trees ripped from the ground, others torn clean in two,
Imagine wah Wild Gilbert woulda do wid mi or you?

Haiti get an Earthquake whey lef thousands dead,
Wipe out couple villages, couple homes, couple sheds,
Up to now dem a suffa from di 2010 disaster,
Ova ten years pass yuh nuh see it massa,
Try fi plan from now so di damage can be less,
Cause disaster wi jus turn up an nyam yuh food
like some wutliss unwanted craven guest!

The Hurricane

The evening chill brought with it a deep thrill of expectation.
In the distance was a gentle hum of the ocean as if troubled by an alien.
Concerns gathered in the minds creating a tsunami-like buzz,
Reminiscent of the last time they were unceremoniously visited.
The inhabitants were not upbeat,
The rolling hills rumbled as if speaking to the obesity or obscene sight in the gathering clouds,
The stately trees still spirited but aged and firm, standing their ground with roots tangled.

The busy docks, will be decked with rubbles and rudders,
The beautiful buildings now providing shelters, workspaces and institutions of nation building is about to be stripped of their titles, and their nakedness exposed,

Soon they will be lashed, broken and untwined by an
onslaught
of discord.

Colourful leaves which once swayed, now rustled, while
others which blew gently, are falling from all angles, all
wrong angles,
all branches parting from trees after being caught up in
this unholy affair,
Before they were attached, loving, living, full of glee,
prospering.

The drought has just been relieved of his post,
But isn't strange how things which once seems so grounded
can easily be moved. How persons once so segregated can be
drawn together by circumstances, how in the midst of such
order there can be total chaos, yet life goes on.

She a creature of nature has arrived, invisible and almost
invincible, made in the air, made of air, descending upon
mankind with wrath, Never listening their pleas, as they
hollered for help but always seeing, keeping a single eye
open for details but never caring enough to see their
distress.

Always embracing rapidly, but not with love, always gyrating,
but to create mischief among men,
She came and spent only a few hours, but took the citizens
and the city's lifetime savings, pride and way of life then
vanish into thin air.

Now, I can speak clearly, she can no longer cloud my mind
with her lawless enchantments,
Indeed many were left broken, bereft of ideas about how
to rebound, some breathless by her kiss of death. Katrina!

Goodbye, good riddance!

Natural Disasters

Natural disasters can happen here or they can happen there,
Disasters can happen anywhere,
Earthquakes, bushfires or volcanoes,
Flooding, hurricanes or tornadoes,
A natural disaster can destroy an entire town,
If a big river overflows, a whole city of residents can drown,
There's really no way of stopping a terrible natural disaster,
So an evacuation plan is what you will need to master,
Remember this a natural disasters can occur night or day,
So be ye prepared! Did you hear what I say?

A Slippery Affair

Citizens unnuh come closer, mi have a mellow drama fi tell,
How a certain tame breed ah Jamaican Pet slide inna oil an gone ah Hell,

Nuh listen to how dem soun or yuh neva ketch di coot,
Nuh watch nuh face either dig inna dem hole like a Fox an find di truth,

Dem say valuable paper dash out, an di birthday an cake sale gwaan well,
Plus yuh nuh need nuh Baccra Masters fi big wuk when barrels ah oil a sell,

Fyah waaarm pon muss-muss tail an gas products always deh pon price,
Suh unnuh gi mi a HR job cause di salary reminds mi of Men and Mice!

Dem Pet yah smooth an slippery eh dem baptize inna rivers of refined oil,
An like a magical Cottonmouth dem wriggle an disappear inna one big coil.

Dear Dad

Its been many a years
but it seems like only yesterday,
when you picked me up for the first time
and wiped my tears away,
Your absence never lasted
the incidents did pass,
What a joyous sound is echoed
when kids say, daddy's home at last!
Seeing to my wellbeing
was always your number one job,
Since birth I'm very please
to call you my dad,
Overlooking the hurdles
staying away from the fad,
With Gods guide, you did
an excellent job,
You provided the best
in ways you knew how,

You took on mountains for us
yet under life's pressures, you never bowed,
You taught strength by being bold
to be helpful and wise,
You left treasures and memories
preserving solid family ties,
I have passed on to my children
virtues learnt from you being my dad,
Because this awesome privilege remains
That only some men will ever have,
To participate in raising
the next generation of life,
Is a blessing with a challenge
but a sacred motivational flight,
Dear dad, you did well
thanks for playing your role,
Your warmth remains in my heart
your advice will never grow cold.

Mother, It's Me Again

Hello mother,
Its me your child again,
Not a favored spouse or a cherished new found friend,
I am saying thank you for your love, and just letting me be,
For keeping your watchful eyes and tender hands over me.

For patience you exhibited, while guiding my first step,
As small as it was, I felt really blest,
You have sacrificed much time by carrying me full term,
Now my life has come full circle and my gratitude I confirm.

Mother I salute you, just for carrying on,
Amidst life distracting noise, your advice hums sweet like a mellow charming song,
For walking so gracefully while wearing a broad smile,
You outshone many stars within a range of a million miles.

You provided me food, even while you had no meal,
You endured daily struggles, but still you kept it real,
You ensured I had drink, while you suffered thirst,
You nursed my wounded body, helping me get pass the worst.

A Queen Is Born

A queen is born,
The first morning I saw you I knew,
Your face, your eyes and your elegant dressing too,
Your words in the wind,
They stroke my weary face,
Your actions so precise you move with so much grace.

I would use all the pages I could buy,
To tell the world about you,
But it would be insufficient to tell of a soul so unique,
So beautiful and so true,
A queen is born in this very land,
I know for sure,
Today I have her hand.

The many times you waited for me,
The concern in your eyes only I see,

To rise above the hurdles of life,
So, I reward you today with a ring to be my wife.
A queen has been born,
This message must be told to the world,
This queen I have found in a very special girl.

Making a Child's Day

Have you ever wondered what it takes to make a child's day?
Lots of funny jokes, toys, and most of all lots of play,
It matters not if it is raining or shine,
All that really matters is that they have a good time.

Listen to them talk, how funny they sound,
It is always a revelation, to have them around,
Look at them dressed, in suits or pretty dress,
Yet very soon, their clothes will be a complete mess,
Some with stripes, some with plaids, others dotted or pleats,
Whatever they wear they will look really neat.

Lots of sleep, lots of snacks and very little food,
Lots of talking, lots of questions, you may even think they're rude,

In some cases you're right in most cases you're wrong,
They're just enjoying their childhood, because learning has just began.

To your child be a good mother, yes, a loving father is also fine,
Work is always hectic but mommies and daddies for the kids find some time,
To hold the little ones in your arms and show them that you care,
They will love you for a lifetime, to their hearts you'll be dear.

The Class

The bell rang,
Off they ran,
Quickly, skillfully, purposefully, compelled,
Together they press in a single file,
Noisy, noisier, noisiest,
Now quiet, quieter,
What happened?
There, it happened
Through a portal they went,
Through that same portal one came,
Obviously, the change factor has taken her seat.

School's in Session

School is in session,
Take in your lesson,
Remember students you are here to learn!

Just do your best,
Master those test,
You got to learn in order to earn.

When time rolls on and ages soar,
You could be disappointed you didn't have more,
So get the pencils out, take up your books,
It's time for schoolwork; it's not about your looks.

I Believe

I believe God has given, to every man his gift,
To make a difference in this world, even a faint heart to lift,
Some I believe are musicians, some I believe are singers,
I believe there are artisans, but all are still winners.

Alas! With all the talents, of which you can think,
There's still not enough talent to move man from this scary brink! The brink of violence, death and decay,
The brink of preventing, a peaceful and brighter day.

Some men were made to build,
while others were to teach,
Some were made for war,
Others to search for peace.

Some to be quiet, others to be loud,
Some for the churches, others to rile up the crowd,
I believe all things were perfect, on that creation day, I
believe it will return, when He will have his say.

God's Promise

If we call out to God, he promises to hear
Like any loving father, you know he is there
Our burdens, anxieties, our pains, our fears
He'll take them from us, just because he cares
Today is that day, so let your voices be heard
From creation its constantly, echoed throughout his word
A promise from God, will always come true
Receiving that promise however, depends entirely on you
Placing blood above your doorpost, or giving up your first born
Covering you amidst the furnace, or sending an angel to warn
Like the plagues of Egypt, killed citizens at will
It's now the Coronavirus, leaving bodies cold and still
Can we be delivered? I know we will
But the end is upon us, prophecies are being fulfill
God promises to lift us, whenever we fall
Today is no different, he's just awaiting your call.

The Gift

His deeds so profound,
His love it knows no bound,
He left it all, to give his all,
He answered loudly humanity's call,

A service so complete,
No angel could repeat,
A love distilled! So pure,
He could give nothing more,

He could give nothing more.

Tomorrow

Morning has broken but like never before
Where is the world going I can't say and I am not sure
What's my response to the cries of the people
Hold firm to your faith though problems are stacked high like a steeple

As the toll of death rises the hopes of many sink
So I say a solemn prayer when of the old, the weak and the sick I think
How did we get here? On the brink of Earth's wrath
By doing our own thing but not really playing our true part

Tomorrow will be different look at the wings of healing rise
For the world there is hope the True Watcher has heard our cries
Peace like a river will flow like melody someday soon
Our smiles will return brighter like the Sun at high noon

Will you be there to see it? I am betting that you will
Because you have faith in humanity and your confidence
intact still

Eternal Hope (The Slaves)

Eternal hope has provided inspiration,
Now it's doing the same for me,
It has strengthened my forefathers,
It has brought them victory,
Against the oppressors, the cruel ones on horse,
Against the ones who came with ships and slaves in irons cast.

Up in the mountains they slept, and hid all day,
Going down to the plantations at nights, they had their say,
Over the obstacles they climbed, and jumped,
Under the bushes laying wait, at times even beside the dump,
Another one is coming! One would shout out,
Another trap is ready! The others would give out,
Down he would go, to meet his maker in the dust,
Up they would rise, shouting, another victory for us.

I Believe I Can

I believe I can,
No matter what they say,
I believe I can,
There has to be another way,
I failed miserably yesterday,
But I'll get it right today,
My failings were just experiences
going over those jagged hills,
Consequences burnt into my memory
Like flaming fires on a massive oil spill,
Now with boldness I can show someone the right way,
Whether family, stranger or a friend going astray,
I believe I can, It only takes the will,
To be a success story, that big dream to fulfil.

Staring at Forty

I questioned the past thirty odd years,
So eagerly I dissected those days like an onion with many rings I sliced through,
With not many wins, I stared at a couple defeated,
Looking deeper I realized I had too many draws with too little ties,
Like a picket fence distractions lined up like soldiers around my twenties,
Foggy on the nature of forgiveness needed to rain on me,
I caressed the thought of being redeemed, even at the eleventh hour,
Could my tiny bronze frame, hold another golden picture?
Will there be another era so flushed with fertile circumstances?
Could I have missed the boat, although I rocked it?
Or, did my ship sail into a peaceful harbor filled with unopened opportunities?

Like rows of matured willows,
I wept as bits and pieces of words and water fell on me,
crushing my deserted spirit under their boulders,
Nevertheless, my antennas are still up,
and whatever the verdict I am securely chained to that result.

Leaves of Life

Green as emerald, yet envied by none,
Exquisite as diamonds, but only treasured by some,
Hated like Ebola, its value accepted like a new name,
Cultivated like a bad habit, others use her trade to gain fame,
Neglected in some discussions like an unwanted child,
Finding no resting place so she took root in the wild,

Her fragrances are well renown,
Her years predates kingdoms and thrones,
Courtrooms and lawyers her virtues discuss,
Her currency is current so her ultimate rise is a must,
Long before recognizing her passion, grade or worth,
Or hearing of her fame, she quietly abided in the dirt,

I sniffed a whiff of her colored hair,
It was awe inspiring I had to give three cheers!

Today you saw little glimpses of her,
Dressed in snow white linen or brown lace as some prefer,
Spun to the rhythm like the rolling fingers contest,
Like a violin her perfume tune rises as she grooves with the best,

Carried by two pillars, while releasing pure fun
Finding a resting place between someone's glossy cliffs or warm gum,
By infectious laughs she disarms and charms,
Earning her place rapidly she grew wildly popular in many arms,
Yet, only to become less visible with each pull on her precious hair,
She gave up her last breath naked disappearing into thin air.

Reflections of a Beautiful Woman

It's cliché but true
beautiful women are hard to find,
So I couldn't believe my luck
when you told me you were mine.
It's not so much your outer glow
but more so your inner mix,
Your poise and phenomenal beauty
that got me so affixed.
Oh how the stars have aligned for me
in every single way,
Presenting you as a unique gift
On this bright and exciting day.
You are an invaluable treasure trove
wrapped neatly in smooth skin,
A sweetly scented bouquet
like freshly cut rose or one just flowering,

You are a stream through the woodlands
nourishing those inner parts,
Like gentle ripples to a pond
you bring movement to my faint heart.
A woman of your class
is born from a special ilk,
Providing life elixir
akin to a mother's milk.
It is good to have met you
Experiencing paths you've always trod,
Still, it's better having loved you
With every ounce of me that I have.
If this poem should be continued
what else would be true?
Knowing that you're loved by the world
Or still knowing that I chose you!

I Do

Can I have this one dance,
The mood is just right.

Can I take these few moments,
If only for tonight.

To tell you how I feel,
To hold you in my arms.

To get closer to you,
There should be no alarm.

For years I have tried,
To secure this first dance.

The price I would pay,
Is a life of romance.

I am ready for this commitment;
I am willing to be true.

Do you have space for two words,
Those words are "I Do".

The Weakness In Me

Tonight I sit and wonder, why am I so lonely,
Why am I feeling so sad, so dragged and troubled as my mind
ticked away hours unending like a new clock,
It is when you run through my mind in your jumpers,
sneakers, with piercing words and sounds,
I have tried to be strong, yes, I have,
I have tried with little success to hold back the tears
associated with the thoughts of you away from me but could not
Is it that I am weak or is it that when I think of you that
I become weak?

Whether the weakness lies in me or it lies in your name,
fame or game and taken with your aim
I want to know,
Since my mind is in captivity to a force of nature,

Maybe I should try to rescue my mind, myself, my thoughts, my sanity,
Or, perhaps it is beyond me and there is no escape.

Why

Why me, why now, why this? Not again!
When will it stop?
Where will it stop?
Who will stop it?

No one can but me.
Stop! Stop! Stop!
Are you hearing me?
Am I speaking to myself?

Do you ever listen?
Why are you so bold, so persistent?
Why me, why now, why this?
I will be asking,
I will be waiting,

I will be listening,
When will you speak?
Just answer me, please why?

A Walk Down Rum Lane

From the watering hole, loud bursts of laughter fled swiftly towards the hills like wild goats,
Few Bats communed but their echoes sounded out of sync,
Cloaked like a nut in its adorning shell,

The lone traveler gripped his spirited pint,
Swaying towards oblivion,
At the corner post he hung on like a broken syllable,
Clutching his crystal crutch next to his bosom,
His newest friend with eyes glittering like a polished gemstone,
Spoke to him beneath the moon.

They chatted for hours as if one would depart soon on the midnight train,
Then suddenly as an earthquake, the thick blanket of joy wrapping them together,

Unfolded like an old scroll,
Exposed to the chill,
His eyes popped wide open
Like two eggs with their sunny side up on a hot skillet,
Grimacing while grinning recklessly,
He entertained himself freely, as he inspected his pockets mentally,
Finding inside dark hollows and pure holes.

I Can't Breathe
(A Tribute to George Floyd)

I can't breathe
Its difficult though I try,
I can't breathe
I hear the oppressed NEGRO's cry,
I can't breathe
To function well my lungs need air
Why does me breathing to you seems so unfair?
I........ can't ....breathe
Though, it's my inalienable right?
I still can't breathe
I'm suffocating from a RACIST chokehold, tight!
I ....can't ....breathe
A devilish knee is pressed against my neck!
I......... can't ....breathe
You're damaging my vital streps!
Why can't I breathe?
Is it because I'm black, you are whack,

I'm pinned down held back, so my life is still under attack?
Check that!
I………… can't……………. breathe ahh!
Injustice is taking my last breath!
Does freedom for my kind or me comes only with my death.

The Precious P's

Push,
Press,
Pull or pressurize purposefully, then pause,
Be patient,
Until you get a plausible result.

Never pull out, part from duty or ease up,
Prevent pulling back because you may just be at the point of success,
When you display a lack of perseverance,
you would then be heading for a precipitous pitfall.

Prophetic papers point to Paul,
who wasn't always a principled preacher,
Remember that first, he was a persecutor,
Perhaps even pundits' proclamations are pale in capturing this point,

Pray like never before,
Persons may be puzzled but,
Prayer is a prime example of penitence on one's part.

Money Is Not Everything

Money is not everything,
So do not allow yourself to be bought,
Money is not everything,
So do not allow yourself to be sold out anymore.

Money is not everything,
Neither can it buy everything as some persons think,
Money is not everything
And for those who believe it is,
They are often taken over the never returning brink.

Money cannot buy peace,
If it could all wars would end,
Money cannot buy love,
If it could no more divorce letters would lawyers send,
Money cannot buy joy,
If it could we would all be living in paradise
And it can never buy life,

If it could there would be no tears in sight.

Money is not everything,
Money will never be everything,
Money cannot get you some things,
No matter how hard you try,
Know this and you're well on your way to success.

Welcome

W: is for worship that is why we are here today, and with joy,
we will worship God in no uncertain way.

E: is for enrichment you will be filled with blessings from above,
as you greet the holy spirit, and fellowship with each other in love.

L: is for a lifetime that's how long we can be friends,
because all through life and even in heaven our praise will never end.

C: is for Christ the living centre of all we do,
Lord we praise you; we adore you, and one day we hope to be with you.

O: is for oneness, it is with this spirit in which we worship

the Lord,
we pray and we sing, we learn his word in one accord.

M: is for the mystery of that great love that god has for us, he remained faithful, humble to death, so in him I will put my trust.

E: is for everyone that encompasses the entire human race, we are happy god had welcomed us, so that we can be saved by his grace.

Angels All Around

I heard the sound of the angels' wings,
I heard their music, sweet songs they would sing,
I saw their harps of purest gold,
I heard harmonies, and stories unfold.

I saw their robes all spotless and white,
Faces shining, they gleamed so bright,
Take me in, let me stay with you,
Cause I've never, felt joy so true.

Can I continue in Earth's long night? After these angels
have taken their flight? "You must return", a voice replied,
Go tell the people, far and wide,
If they like you, will faithful stay,
Then they with you, will be taken away.

This Must be Paradise

I heard the sound of the angels' wings,
I heard their music, holy songs they sing,
I saw their harps of purest gold,
I heard harmonies, melodies untold.

I saw their robes all glittering white,
I saw their faces shining oh so bright,
And holiness filled the air,
Holiness filled all the air.

Please take me in,
Let me stay here with you,
I've never felt love so true,
How can I stay in Earth's dark night?
Now that I've have seen this life-changing light.

"You must return", a voice replied,
Go tell my people far and wide,
I will return to whisk them away,
To live with me in endless day.

Three Time's the Charm

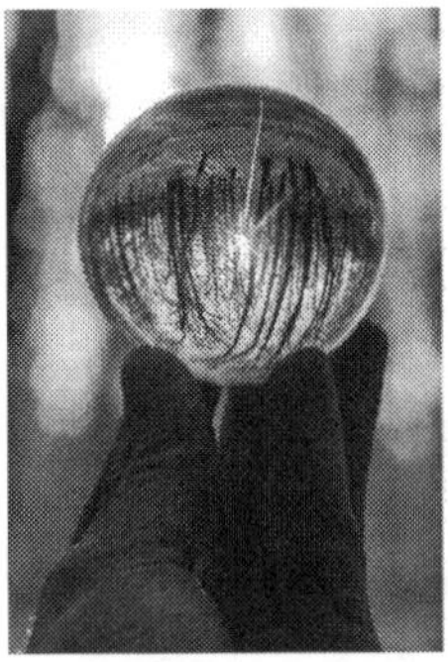
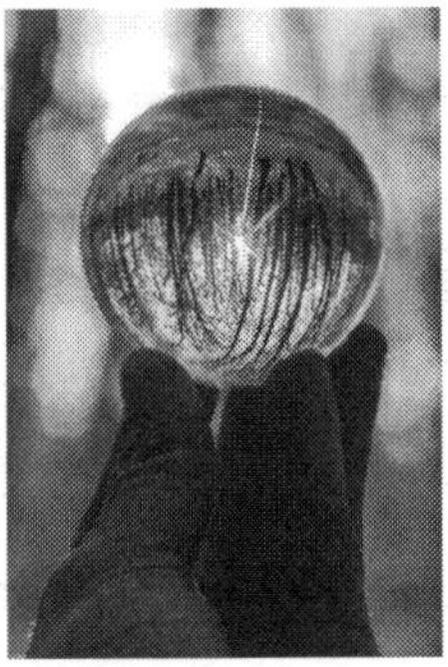
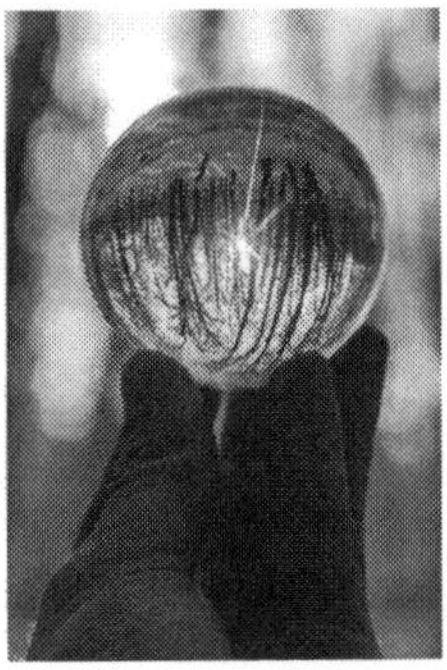

Three times is the charm. Is it? So they say,
It's like the good, the bad and the ugly,
The Indians, the cowboys and the outlaws,
Yes, no, maybe, are still valid answers that will work whether,
here, there or somewhere.

Can it really be that you must have it, all of three times
to be lucky? If so, why is the number three considered an ominous sign and associated with death?
Why is it that if you try and fail, you should try and try and try again?
Did you notice that it was three times that your patience should forebear?

Can you tell me why the colour of the French flag; blue,

white and red?
Or why is the colour of the Italian flag; green, white and red?
Why was a certain Ethiopian king crowned three times?
And why is their flag also tricolor; gold, green, red?

It really seems that three is the charm, really, is it?
So we were made to live, then die, and then live again?
Why are there land, sea and air?
Now I have read about Heaven and Hell, is there an in between? Why do we classify things and persons as good or bad, can't there be a middle ground?

Who knows, only The Father, The Son and The Holy Ghost.
I always thought that in a conflict you didn't need to take sides,
So why take a position left or the right, when there is always a neutral position?
What do you think?
Can't matches be won, lost or drawn?
Why are there always three sides to a story or a triangle?
However, when the triangle is made around a love story it normally has one result, not three.

Have you heard about this beautiful island, and the Caribbean Sun?
Where you'll find laughter, sand, sea and lots of fun,
If you search diligently you, may even find me,
Lounging at dusk, under a coconut tree,
Cornwall, Middlesex and Surrey points to the divisions we endure,
But the black, green and gold tells you even more.
Three time's the charm! Is this concept new?
I am still not sure, how about you?

Coloured Views

So green the leaves,
the shrubs, the shoots, the grass,
The paper chased by many in this world,
Although it never lasts,
The envy eating away
at the heart of many souls,
leaving them white and dry like old sepulchers,
So orange the sun,
the sweet fruit, my new boot,
So black, my hair,
the tar, my pants, my car.
The last bottle I saw when leaving that bar,
Oh so blue,
so blue the sea, the sky the flower I like,
the stories I tell,
yes bluebells,
The way I feel when you are away,

the way I think this world should be coloured,
Peace,
calm,
universal bliss.

Although Far Away

Although far away
I feel at home each time I hear your name,
Seeing your fame has done little to reward or massage the longing that burns in my soul,
Dreaming of tomorrows that I know will never come,
Me I am overcome, because I'm worlds away from the land of sea and sun.

Although far away
I hold dear memories of my youth,
Flickering flames danced in my backyard
with the fragrant smoke of friendship always rising from the blaze,
Ripples of joy, running down the lane,
whenever the weekend starts,
Never alone again I think, like Christmas gifts on a holiday carts.

Although far away
We listen for your ever beckoning call,
Like the weeping willow your sound is lost in the forest,
but unique to our ears,
If one day we should travel, it would be back to you,
Nowhere else on this earth, could we be happier,
because although gone, we are always in love with you.

Note: JCDC: Jamaica Cultural Development Commission

Glossary
(of Jamaican Words/Terms)

Ah	A
An	And
Baaba	A person/anyone
Bangarang	Uproar, upheaval
Barra	Borrow
Bawn	Born
Behavah	Behaviour
Bess	Best
Bole	Bowl (Cricketing term)
Bout	About
Brap	The sound of falling hard/quickly (Thud)
Bredda	Brother
Bruck	Broke/Break
Butta	Butter
Bwoy	Boy
Caaaan	Can't/Cannot
Chatta	Chatter
Chatta-box	A person who talks a lot
Cooh	Look here
Coovah	Cover
Coulda	Could have
Craven	Greedy
Cyaan	Can't/ Cannot
Dat	That
Dawdi	Daddy
Deh	That
Dem	Them
Di	The
Di Rock	Jamaica
Dutty	Dirty
Faamah	Farmer

Fadda	Father
Fambily	Family
Fass	Fast / Curious
Fi	For
Fiwi	Ours / For us
Fren	Friend
Fyah	Fire
Galang	Go along / Go away
Grung	Ground
Guh	Go
Gwaan	Go on
Haffi	Have to
Hav'	Have
Hol'	Hold
Inna/Innah	Into / In
Islan'	Island
Jus	Just
Kin	Skin
Kine	Kind
Kum	Come
Lef	Left
Likkle	Little / Small
Luv	Love
Lyfe	Life
Madda	Mother
Mass / Massa	Mr / Sir
Matta	Matter
mawmi / mawmy	Mother
Memba	Remember
Merica	America
Mi	My / Mine
Muss-muss tail	Mouse tail
Miself	Myself
Naaw / Naw	Nay / Not/ No
Neighbahood	Neighbourhood
Neva	Never
Nexx	Next
Nuff	A lot
Nuh	No

Nyam	Eat
Ole	Old
Ongle	Only
Outta	Out of
Pawdi	Partner/ friend
Paypah	Paper
Pickney	Child / Children
Pon	On
Pure skin	Gum
Regula	Regular
Roun	Around / Round
Settin	Setting
Si	See
Sista	Sister /Sistah
Soso	Bare/ Without a thing
Soun	Sound
Stan'	Stand
Suffa	Suffer
Sugga/Suggah	Sugar
Suh	So
Tek	Take
Ting	Thing
Tru	True
Trute	Truth
Tuff	Tough
Tun	Turn
Unnuh	You all
Unnuhself	Yourself
Waaarm	Warm
Wah	What
Whey	Where
Wi	We
Wid annadah	With another
Wonda	Wonder
Worl'	World
Wutliss	Worthless
Yaad	Yard
Yes I	Rastafarian jargon for agreement
Yu / Yuh	You
Yute	Youth

The Author's Thoughts

Thoughts on my book, **Coloured Views.** This 'likkle' book contains good work. Using a wide array of themes and expressions from the Jamaican culture and language, in addition to my personal musings, I present you a gem. A book for everyone.

All the poems were penciled around sobering views, mixed to touch the emotion. The book's aims to entertain, develop, inspire, motive and stimulate the creative side of the reader, while simultaneously outlining and exposing them satirically to the Jamaican reality.

This collection of poems would make a great gift for the home, a visitor, or for a family or friend abroad and it could be a worthy addition to a library for literature or poetry classes.

Read, share and enjoy.

Made in the USA
Middletown, DE
23 April 2024

53383084R00057